I Love Art!

Book 2
I Can Draw Friends

Illustrated by Krystal B. Liburd

Prologue, Comments and Helpful
Hints by
Faithe Reid-Liburd, M.S.

Published by Faithe Reid-Liburd

Printed in the United States of America

ISBN-13:978-1499536461

ISBN-10:1499536461

—

Prologue

Children should be exposed to art when they are young. Art can be used for play time activities and at any time during a child's development. Although schools are primarily focused on children passing standardized tests, I hope that they will not neglect the Arts. Our children need them.

In book 2, you will see the continuing progress of this artist. These are pictures of friends just being friends and having fun. Enjoy viewing these pictures and creating some memories of your own.

Faithe Reid-Liburd, M.S.

Introduction

From the time that I was a child, I loved art. I wanted everyone to see my art in all of its stages. I hope that this book will encourage other beginning artists.

Thank you for taking the time to read my book!

Krystal B. Liburd, Artist

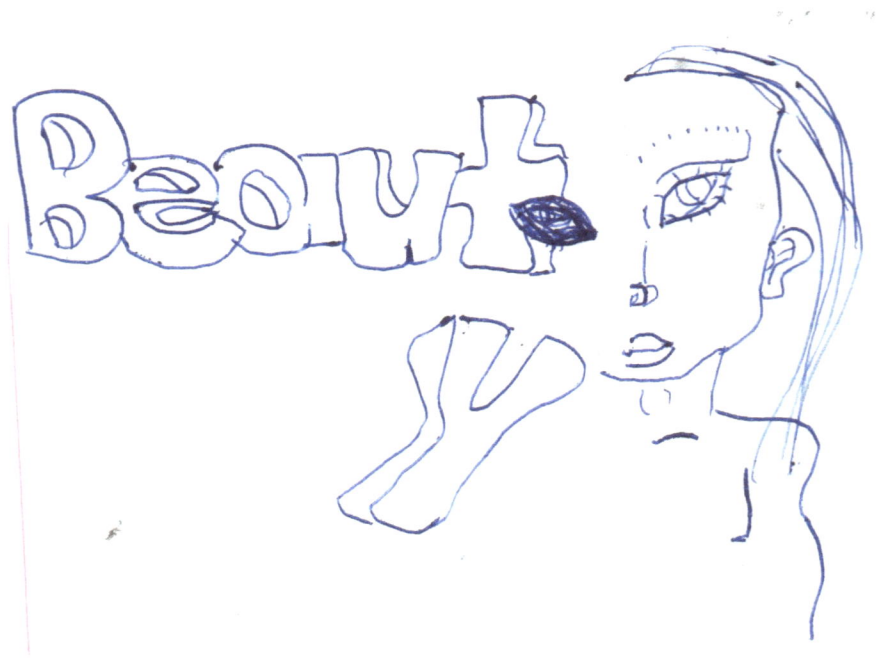

I Love Art!
Book 2

I Can Draw Friends

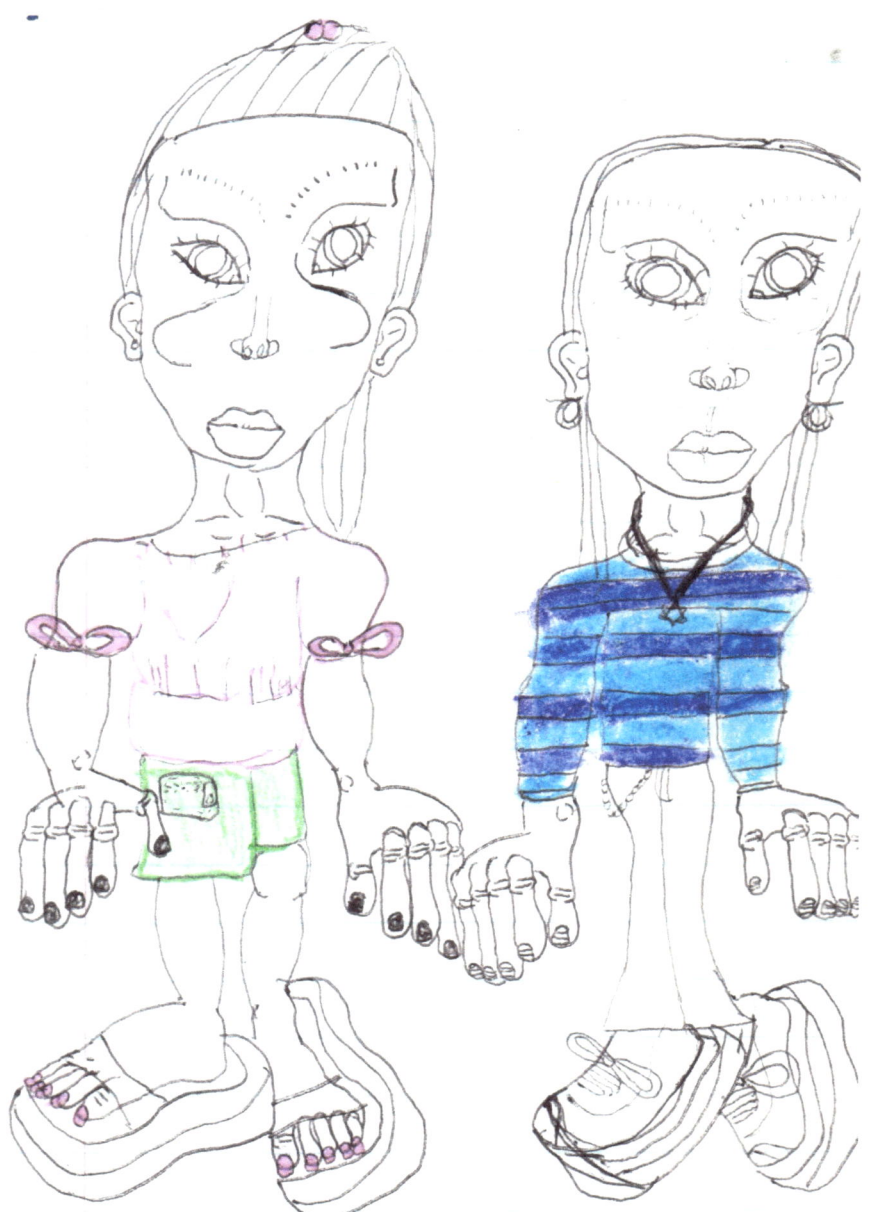

Best Friends

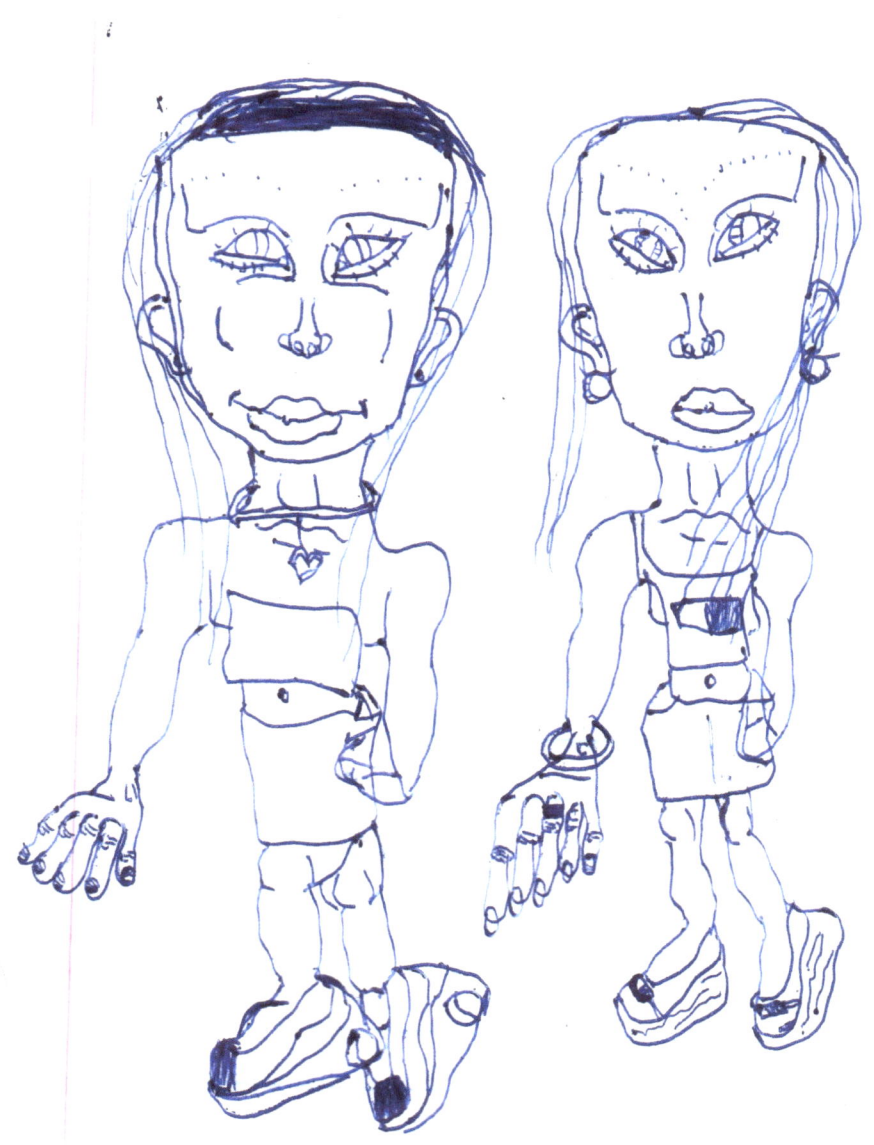

Just stepping out……

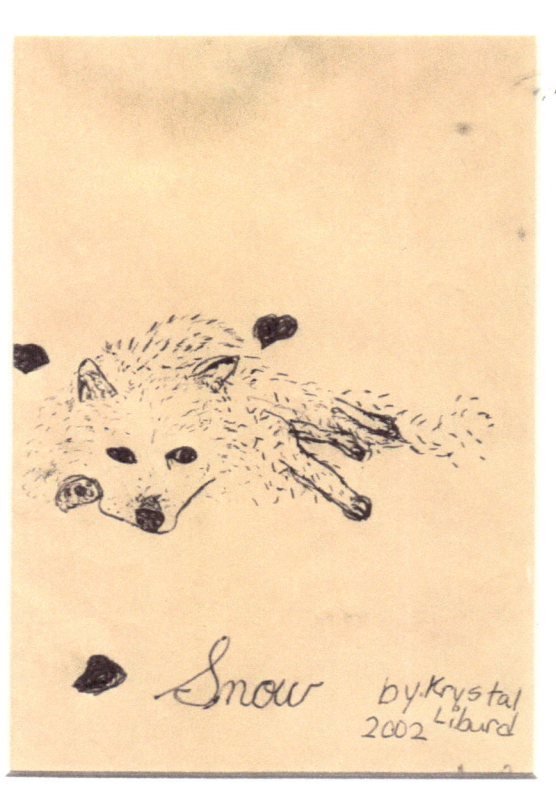

My cousin's pet

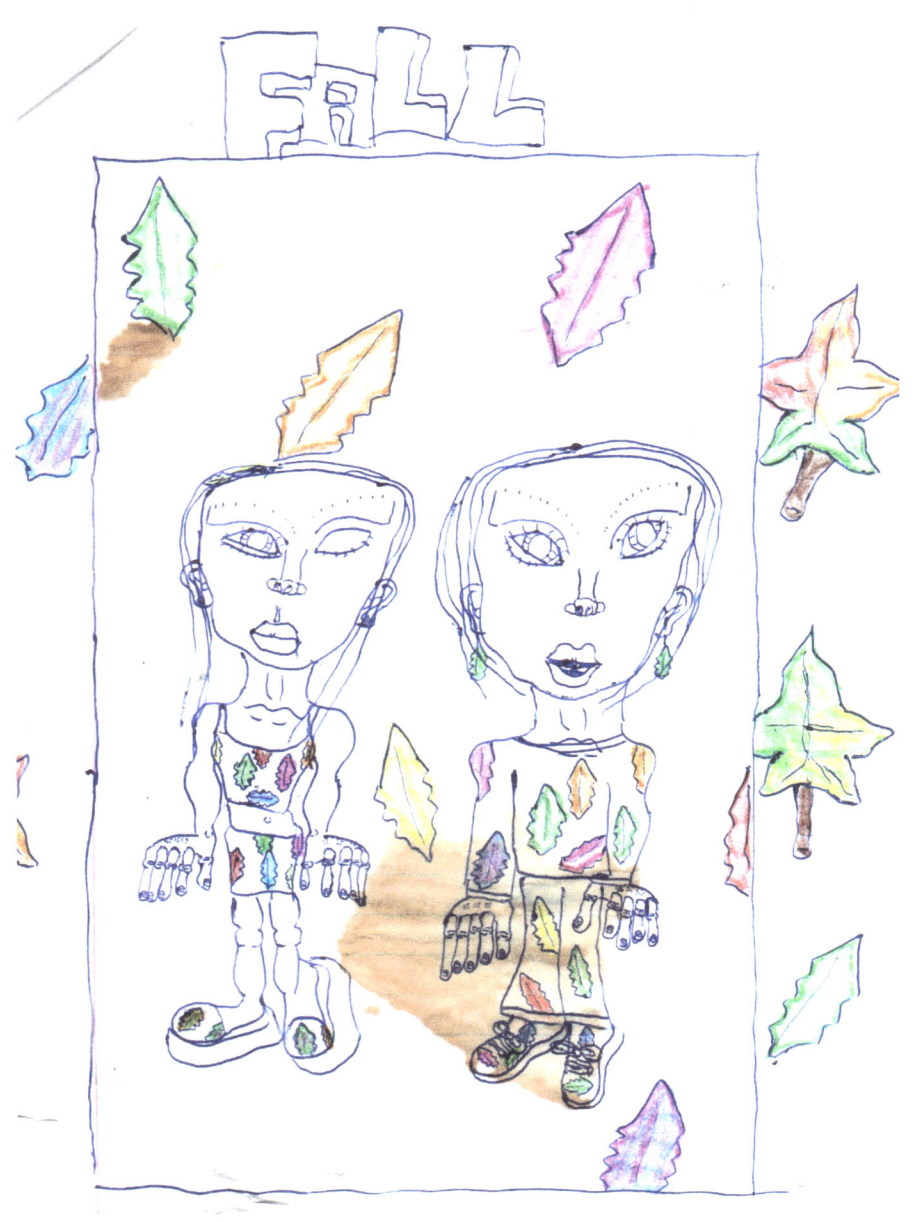

Having some fun in the fall

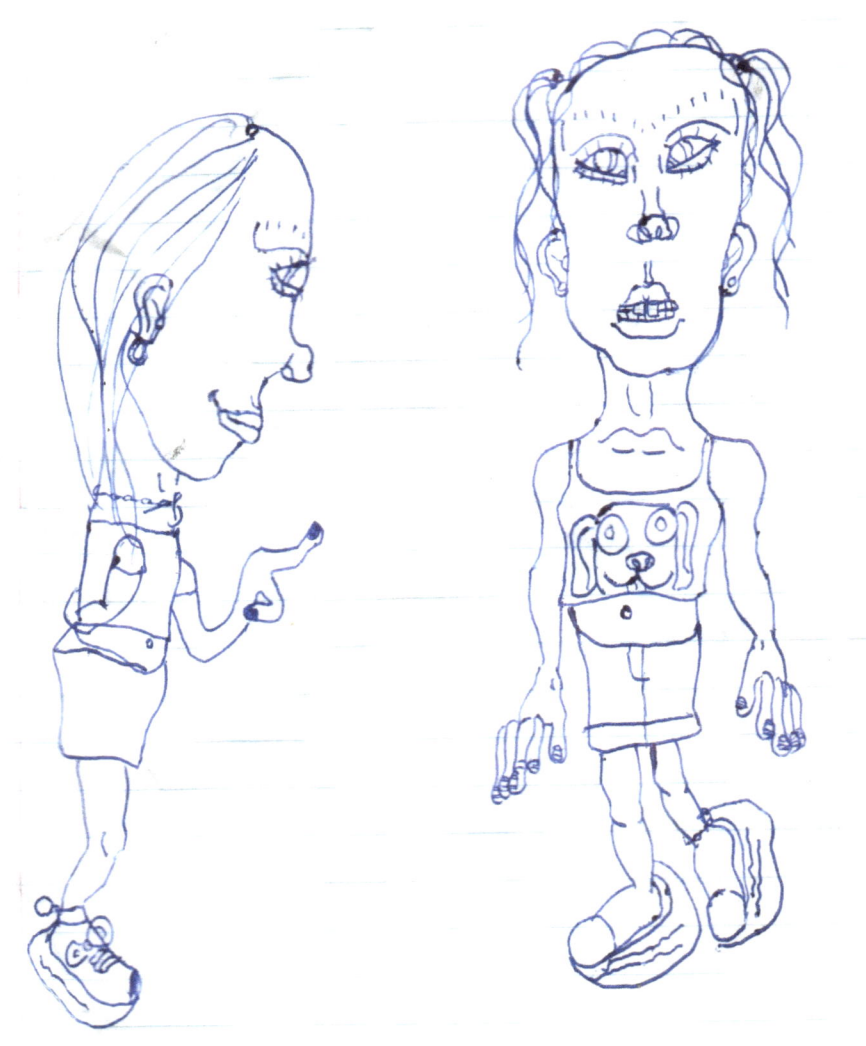

Don't do that!

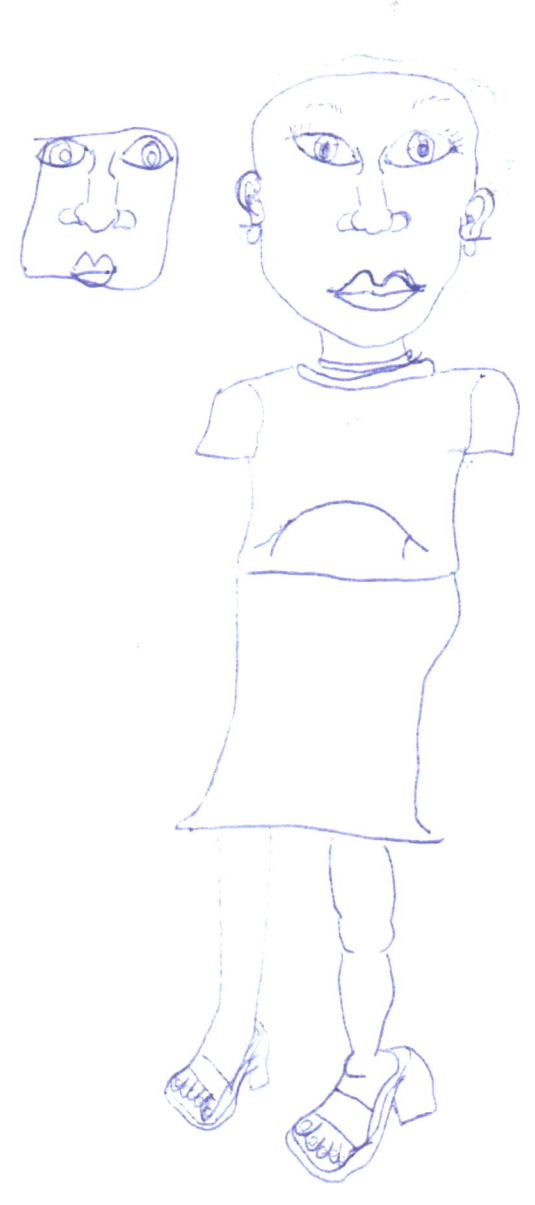

Can you finish this picture?

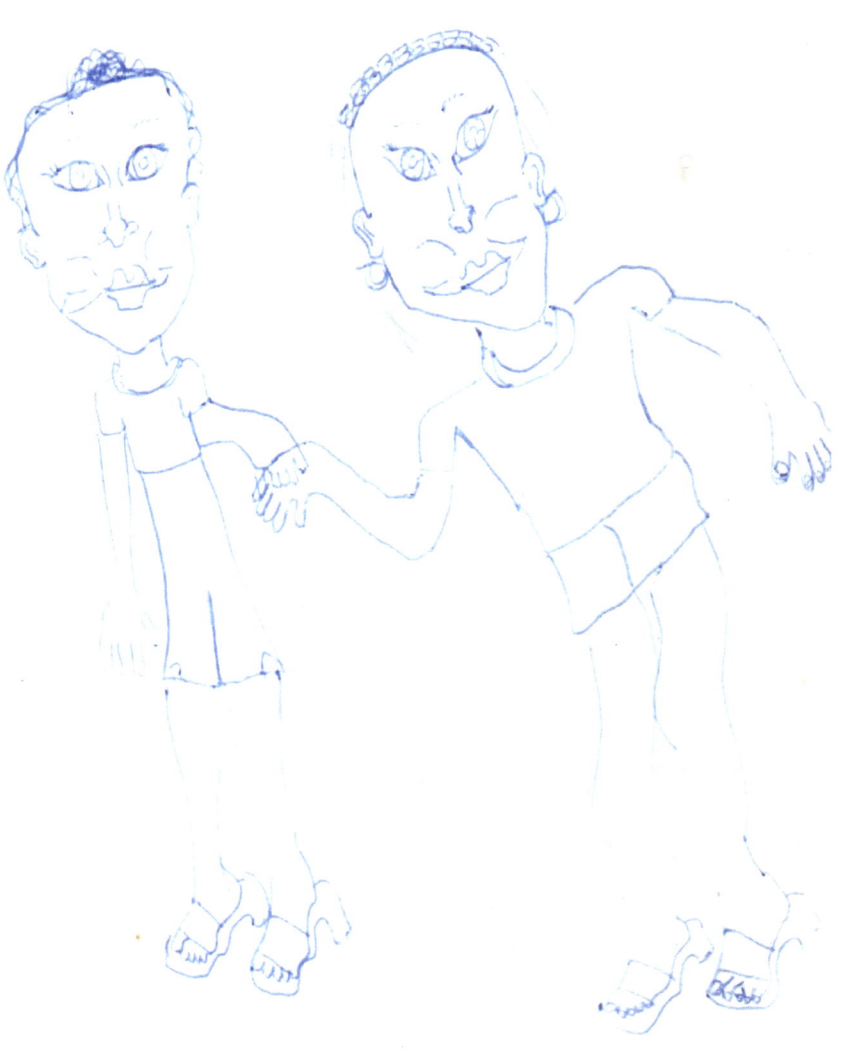

Let's go……

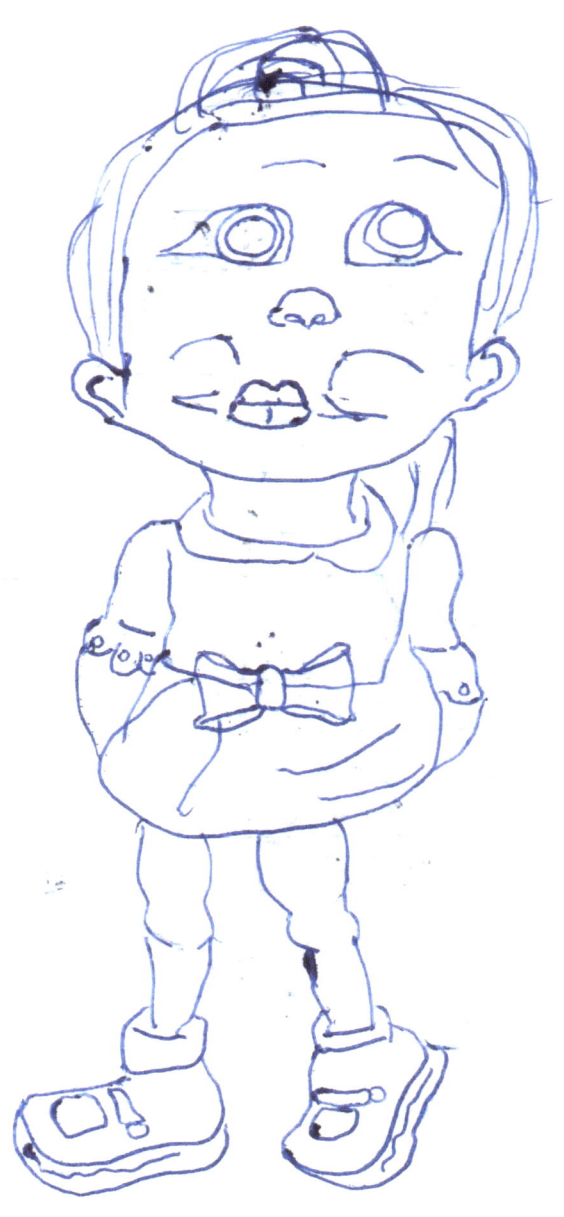

I can be your friend.

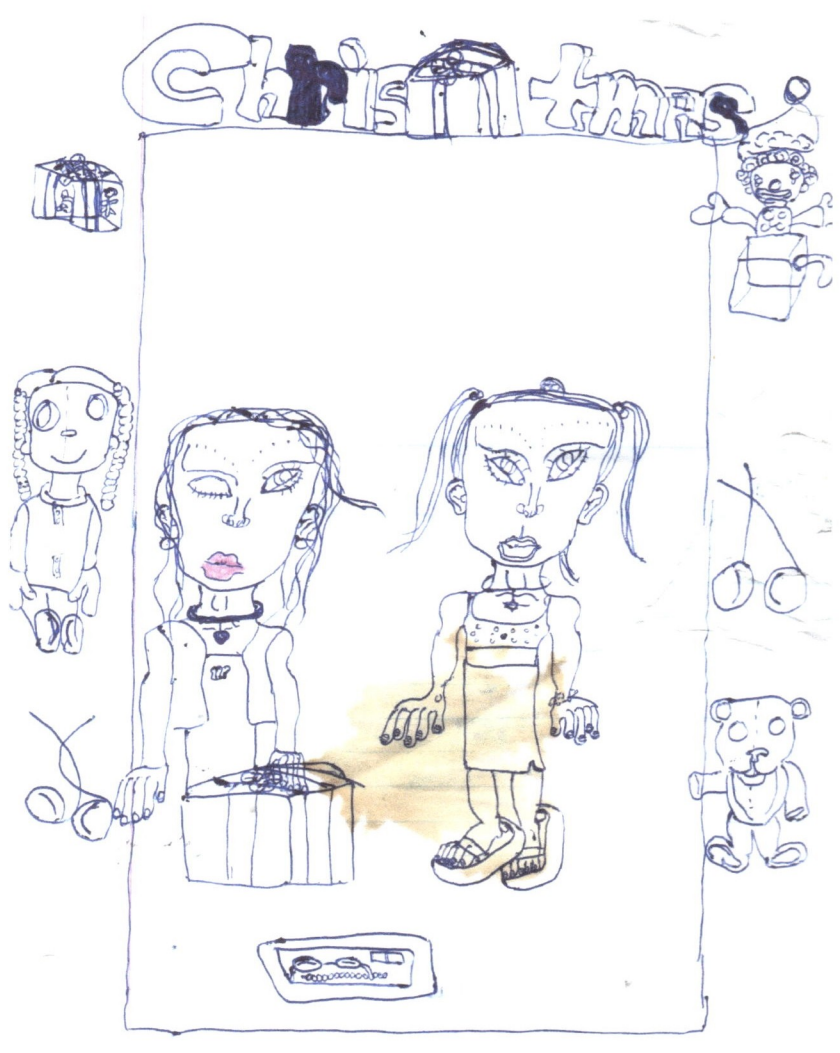

Christmas is a great time of year….

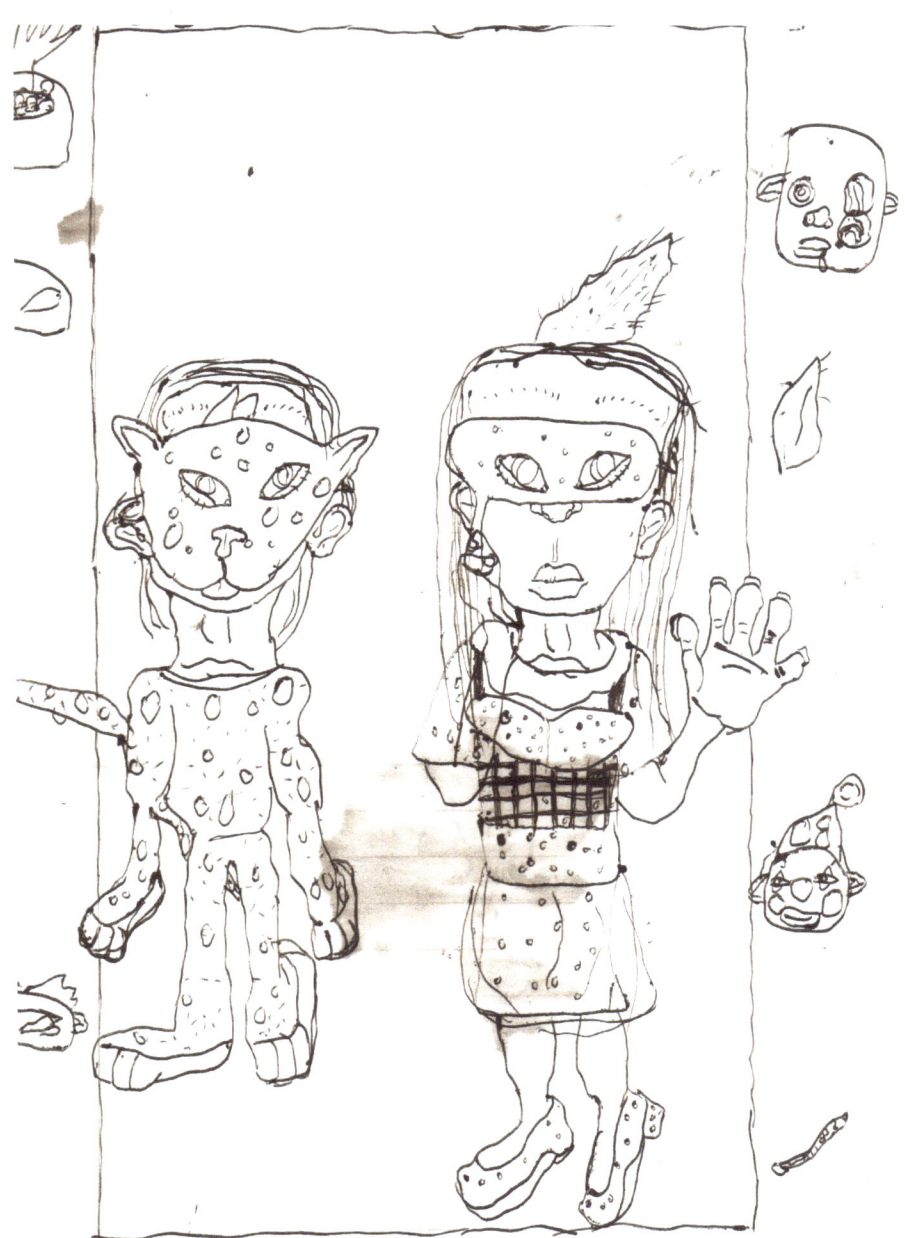

It is dress up time in our favorite
costumes……in Sepia Antique…

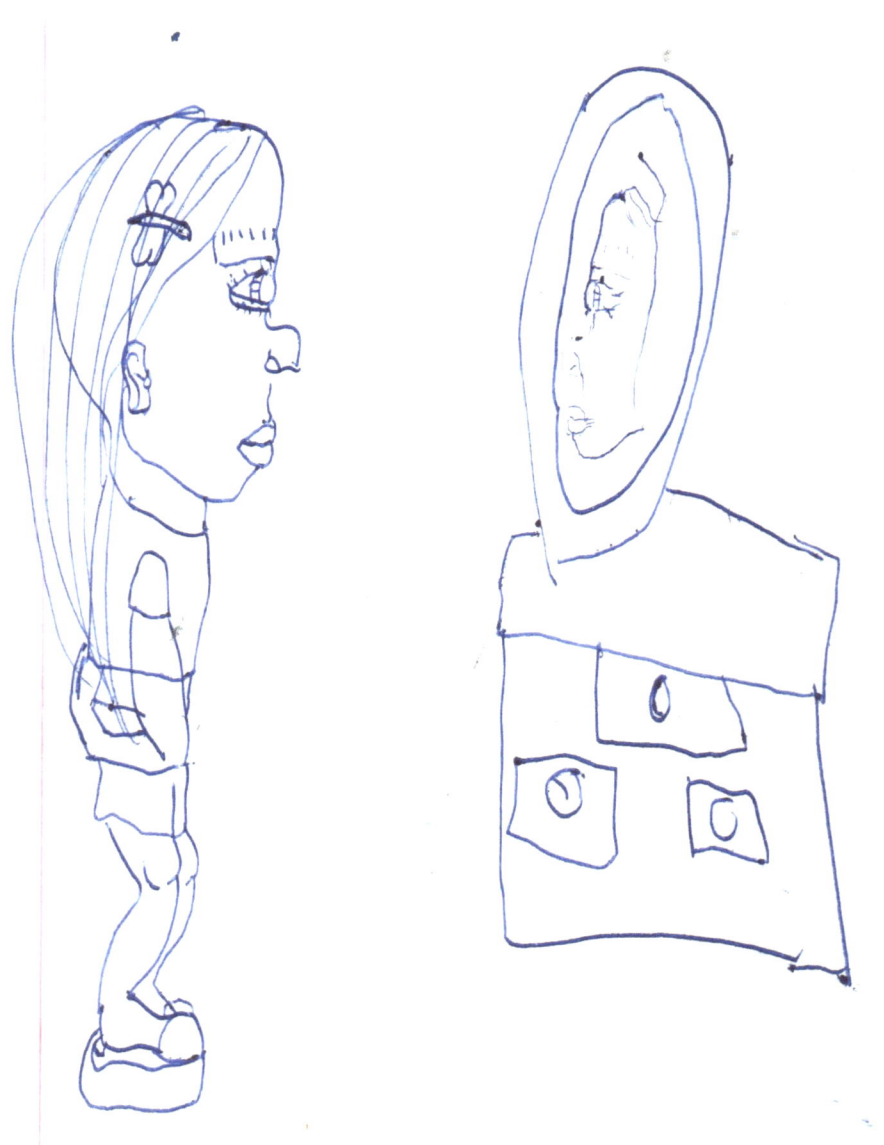

I am beautiful!

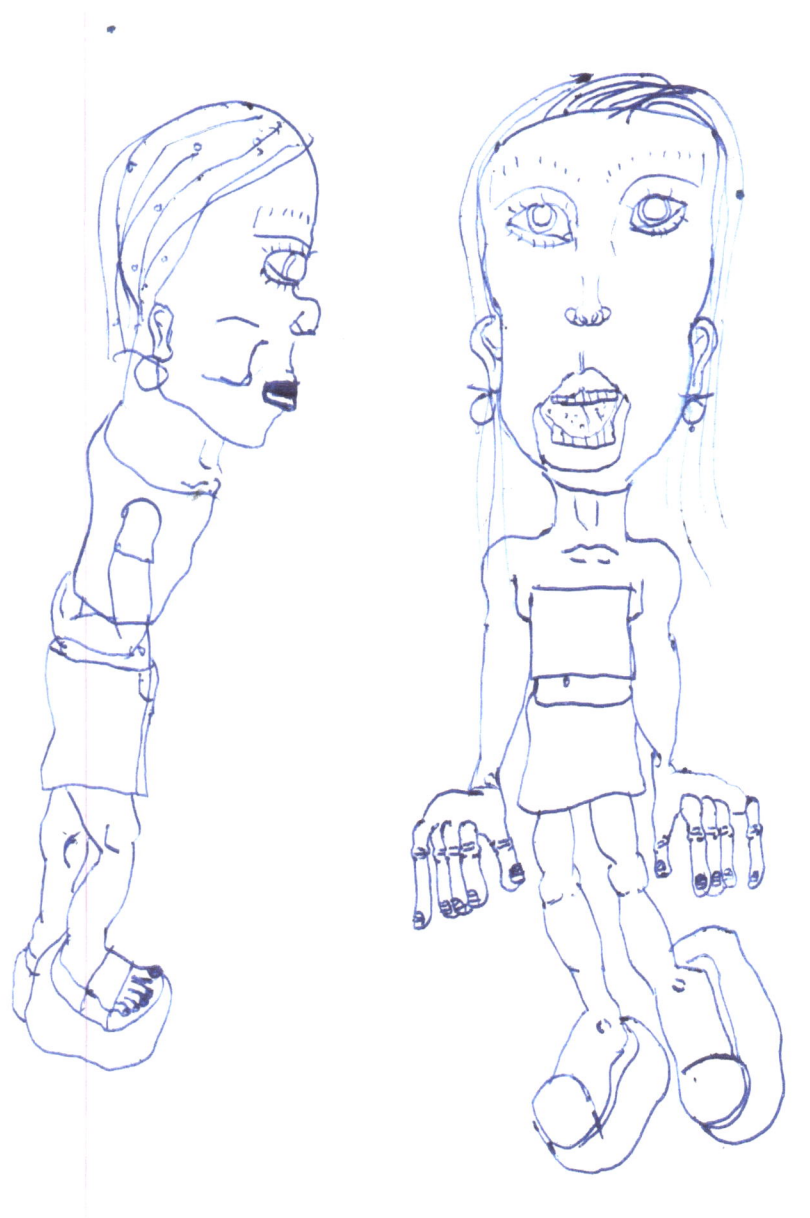

What were you saying?

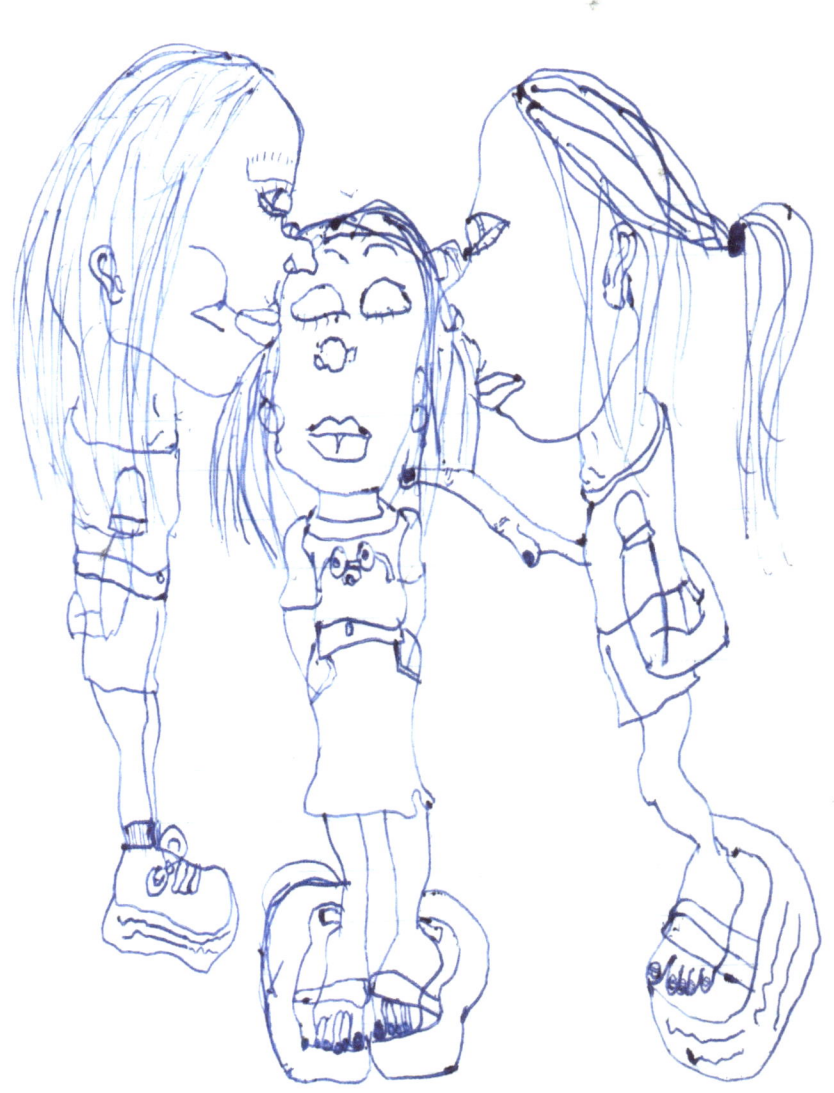

I am loved.......

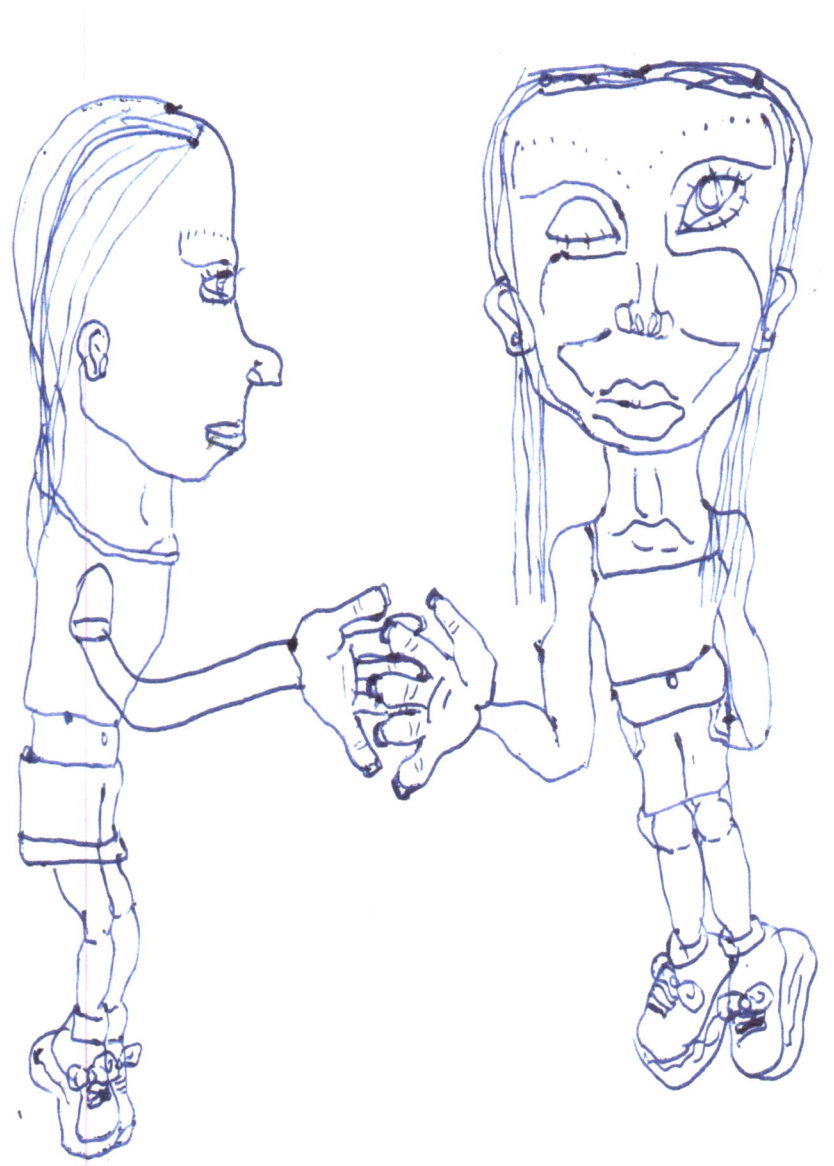

This is how we do it.....

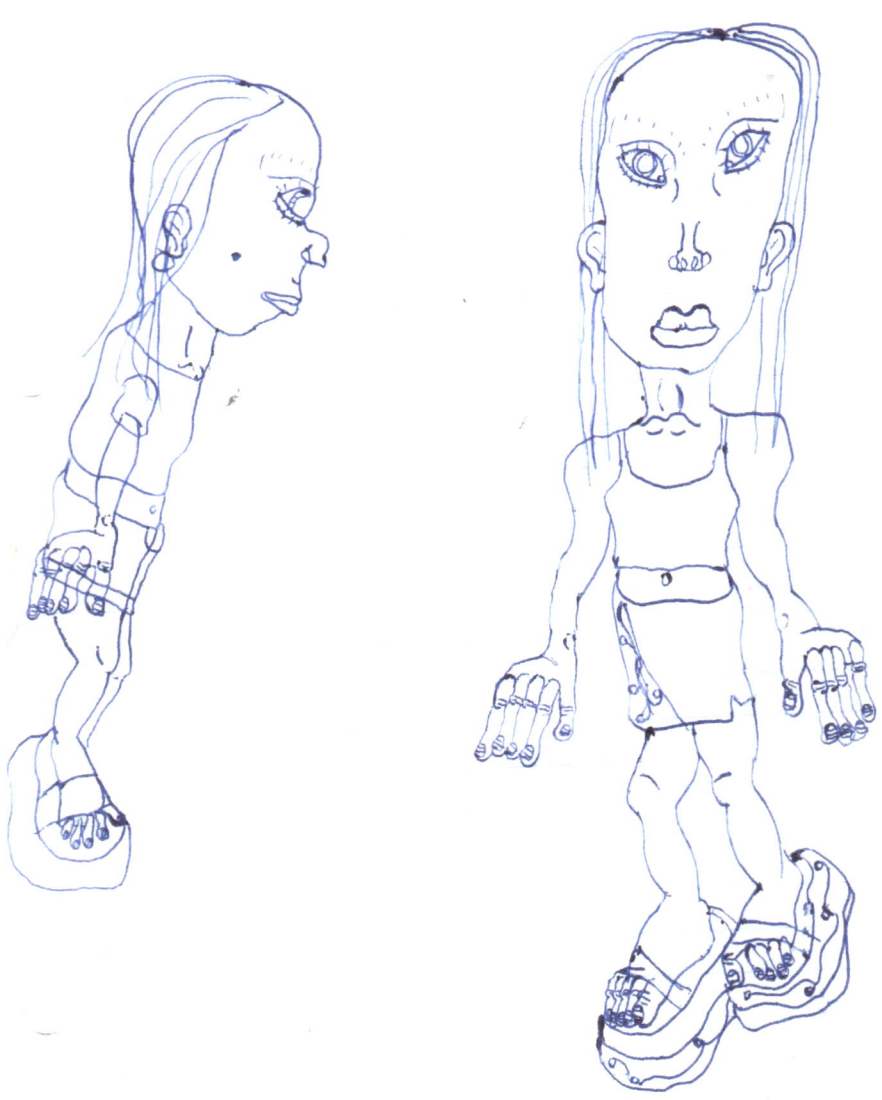

We need a trampoline!
We love jumping up and down!

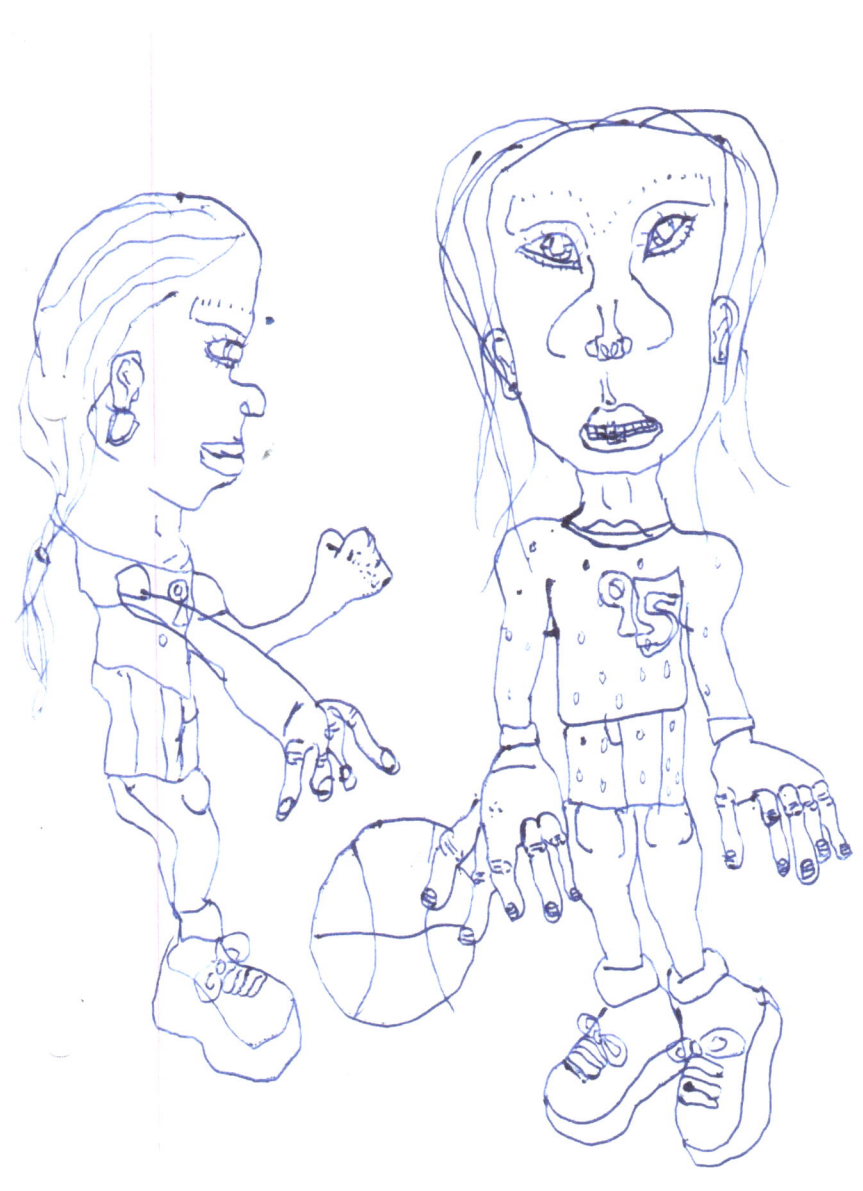

Playing ball is fun.
Get up and exercise!

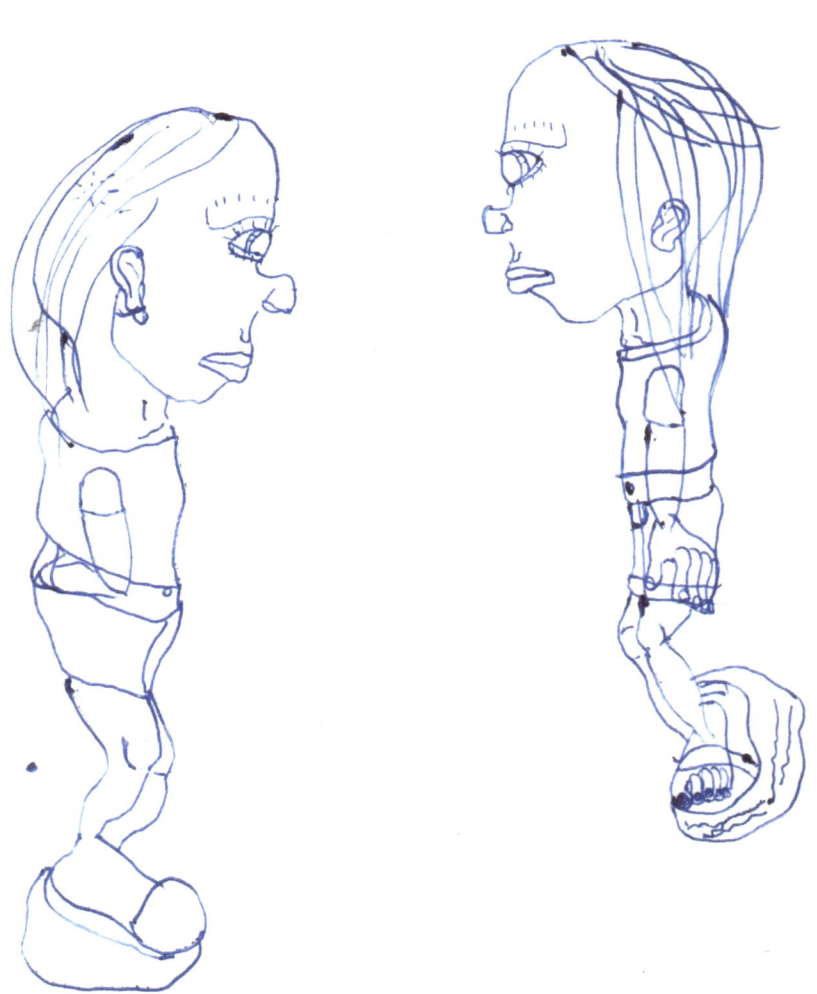

Where's the jump rope?

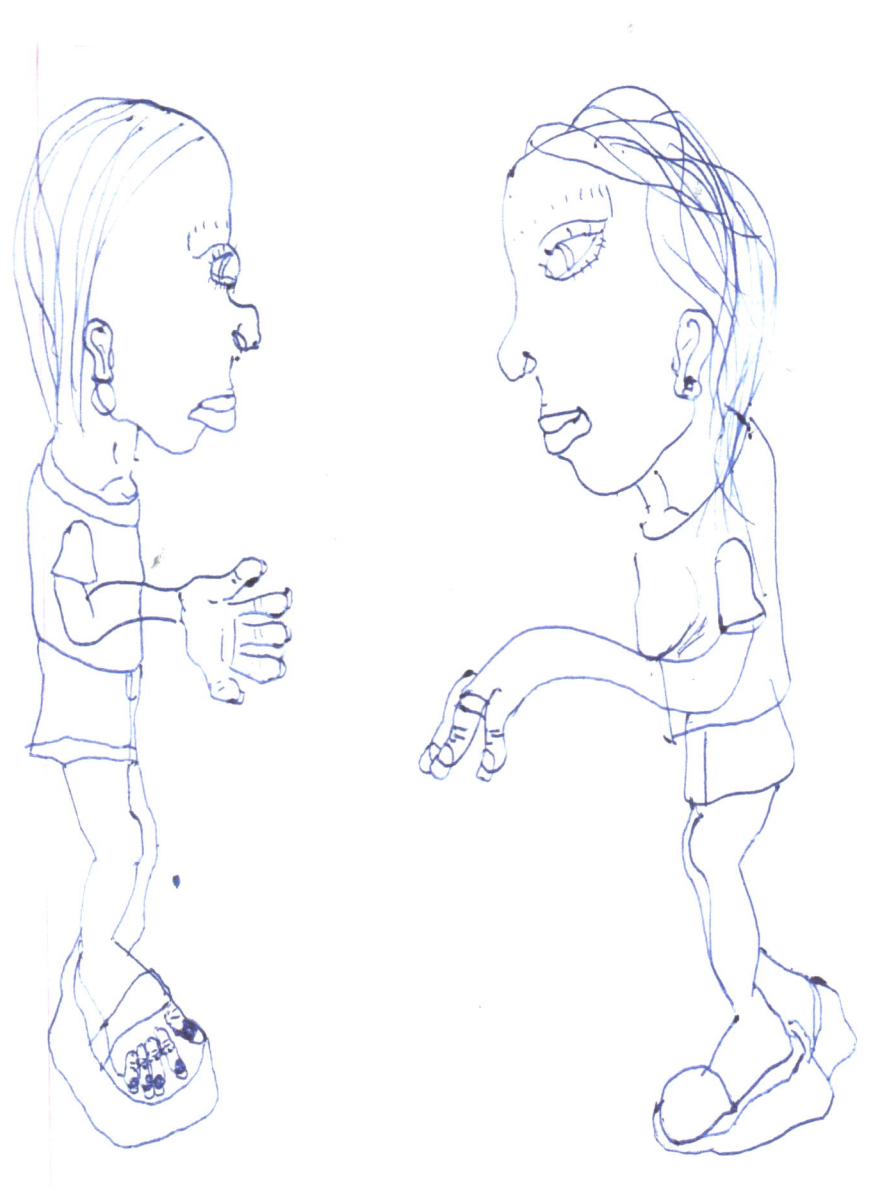

I need your help.

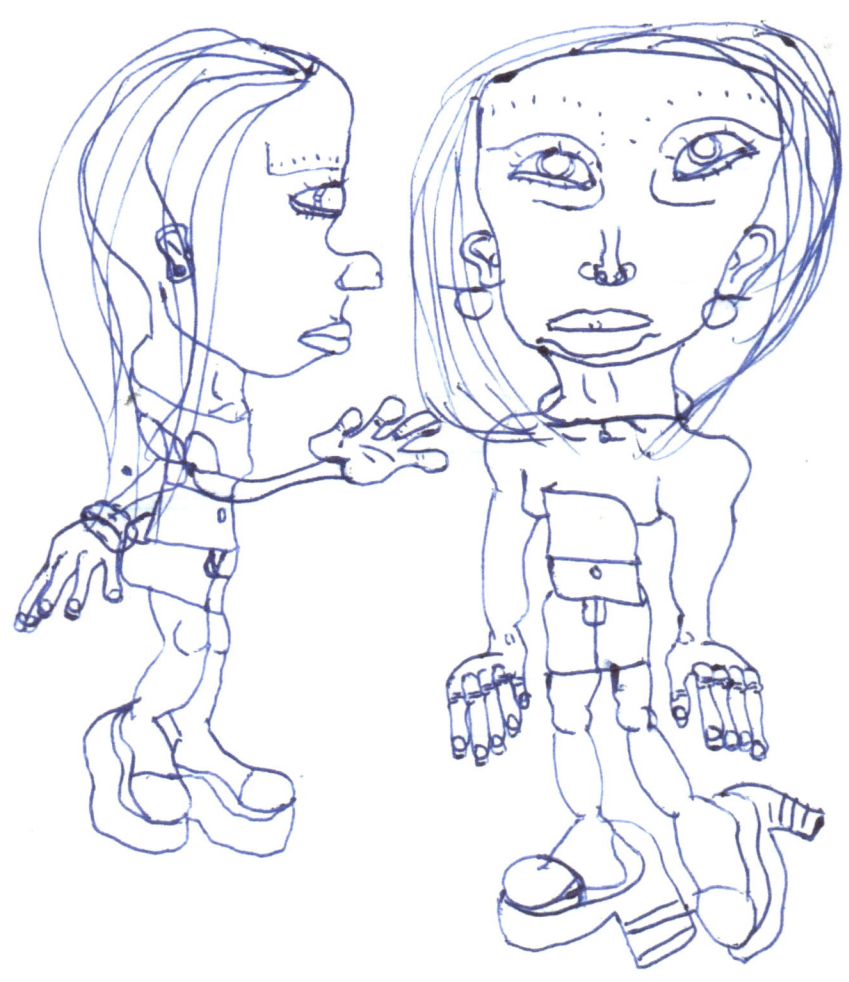

I need to tell you something.

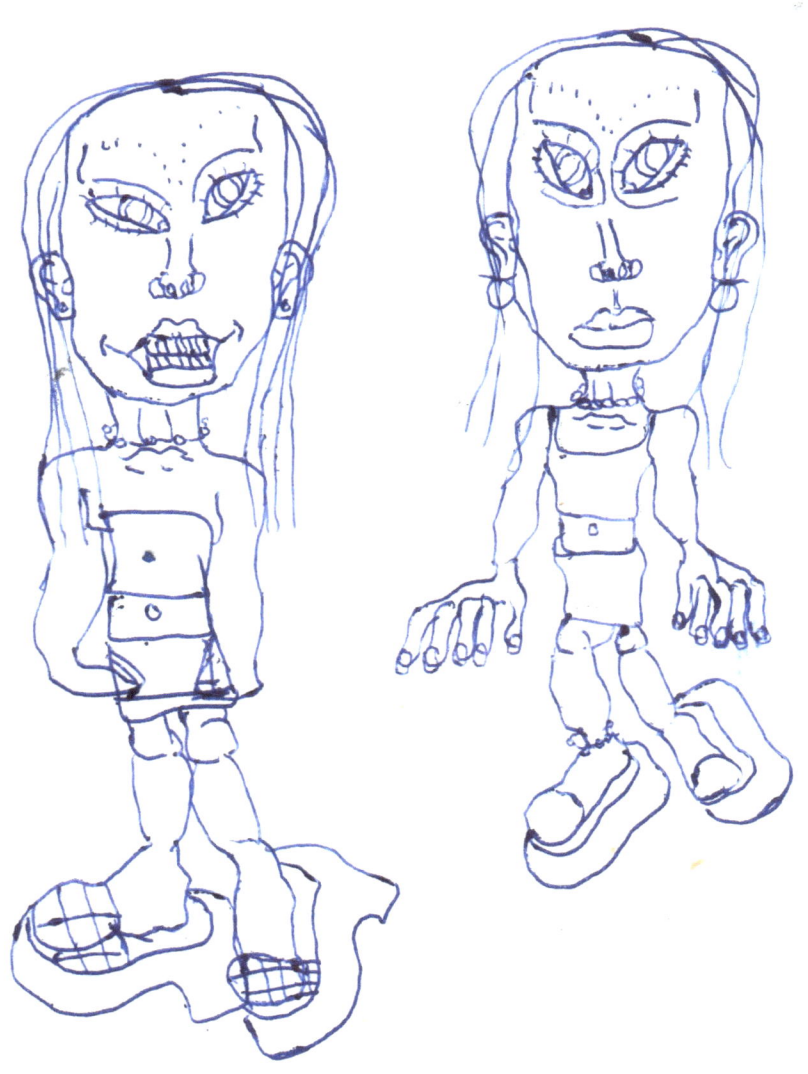

Do you like our shoes?

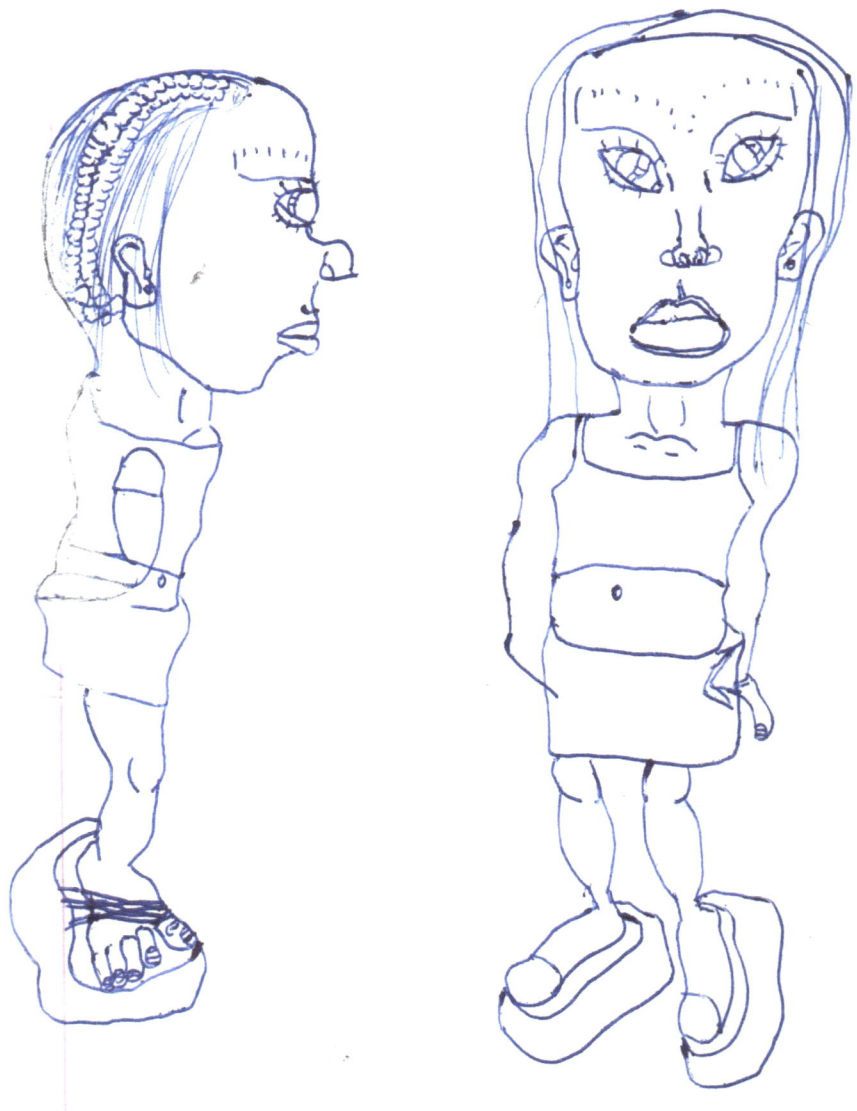

Don't look, but he's coming this way!

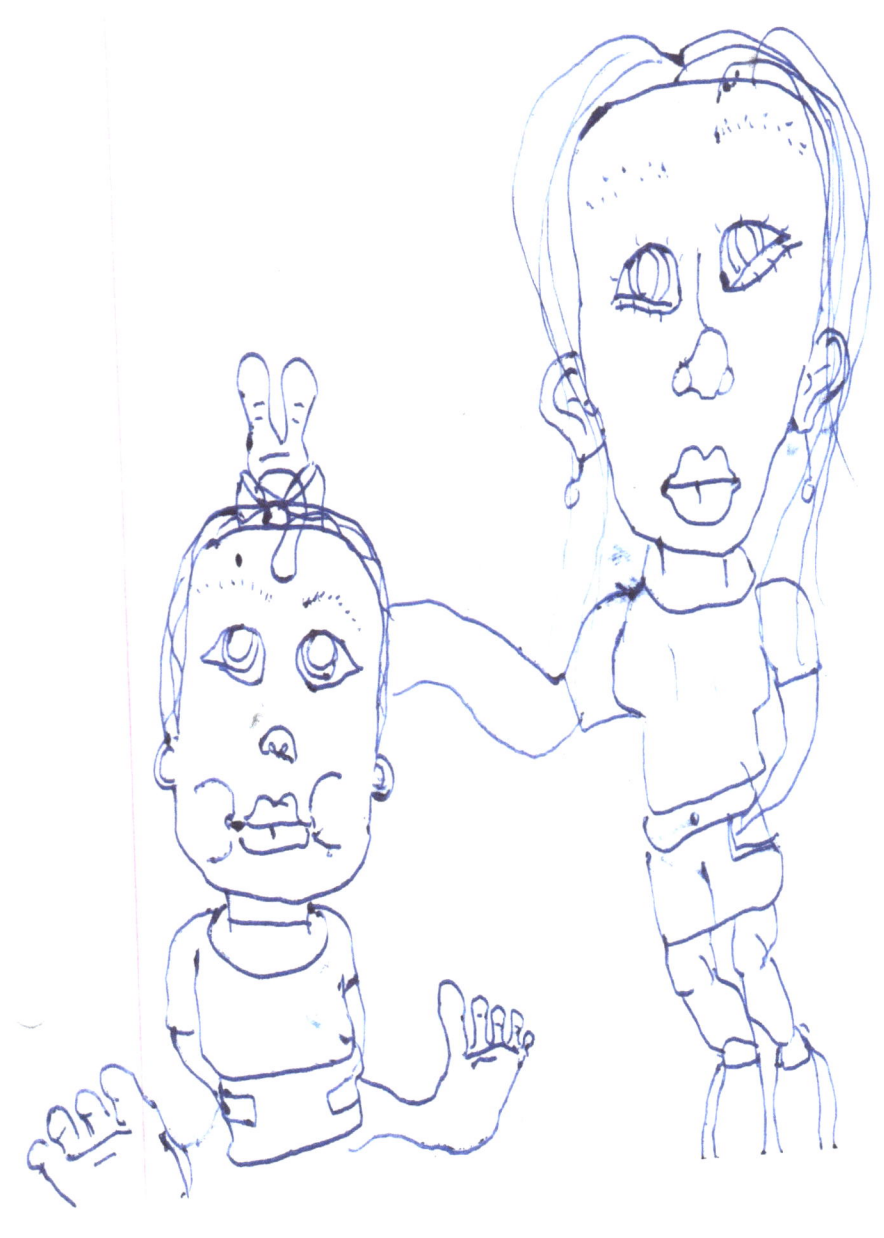

My little sister is my friend.

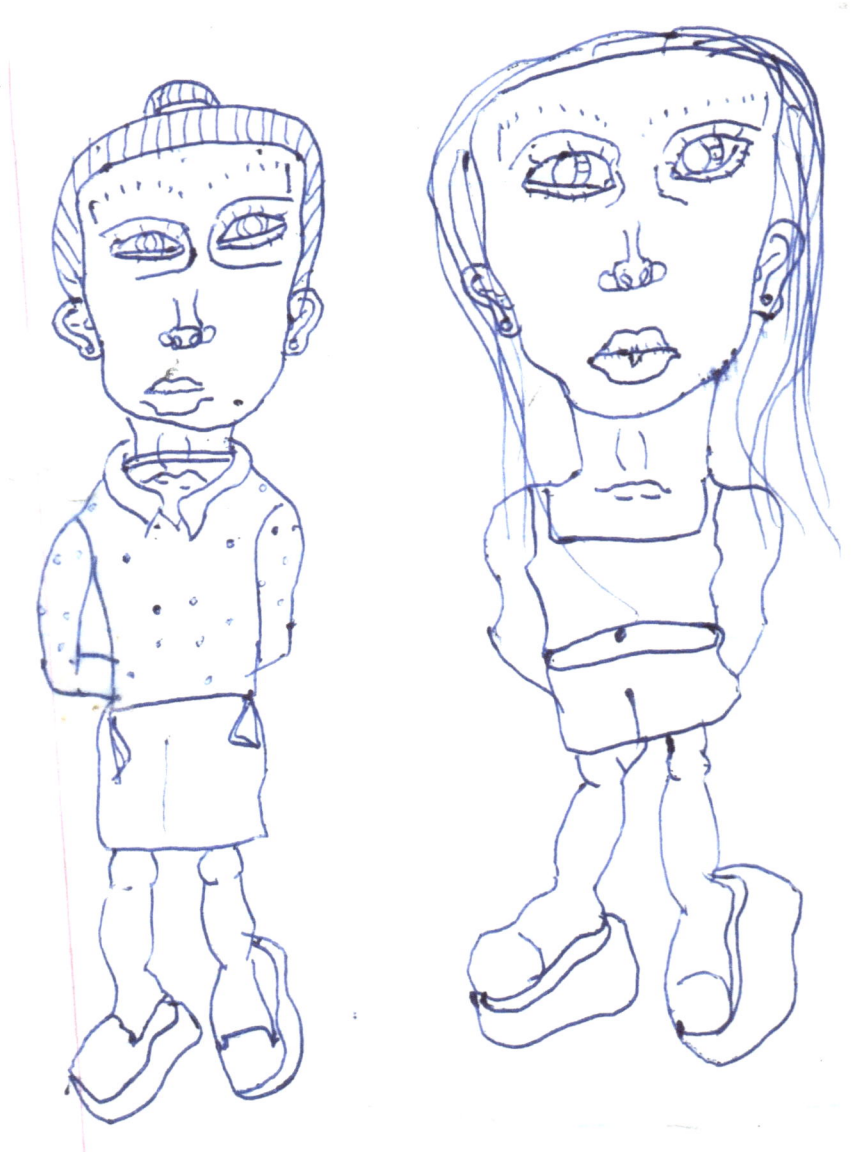

Every thing is fabulous!

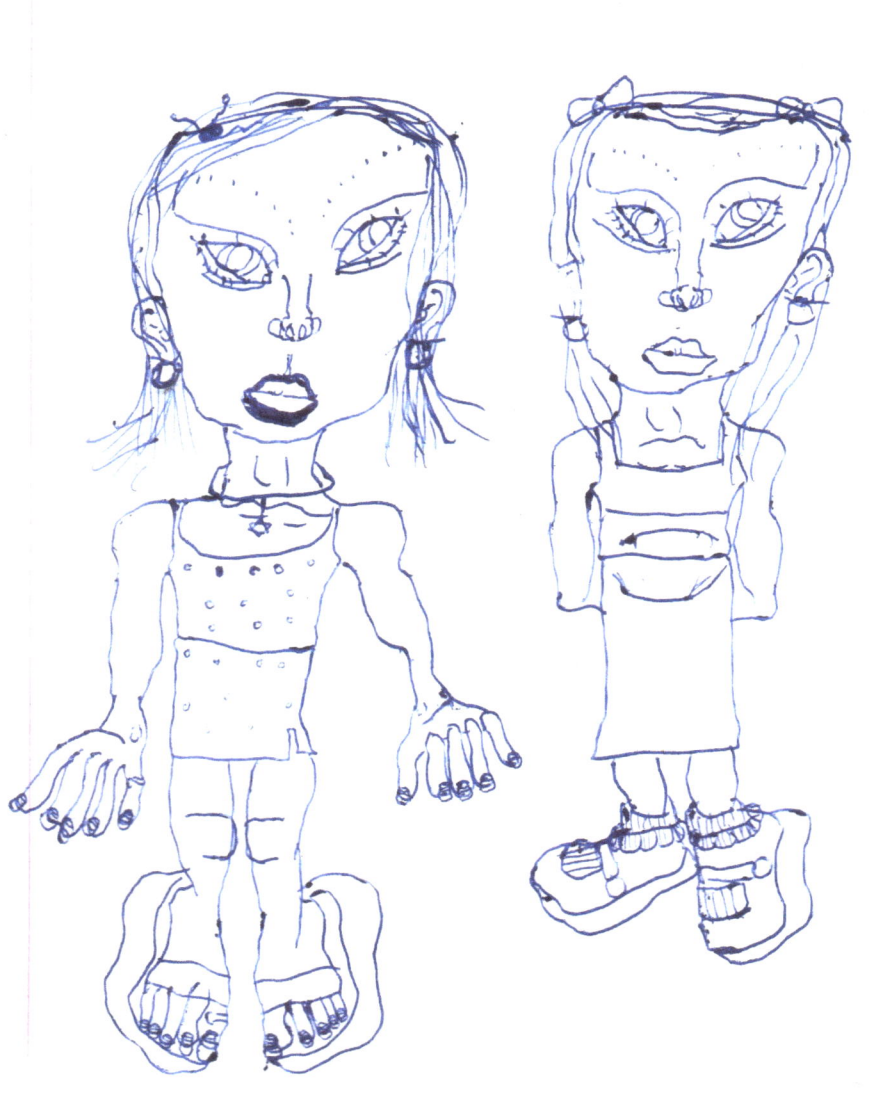

Step back! I just got my nails done!

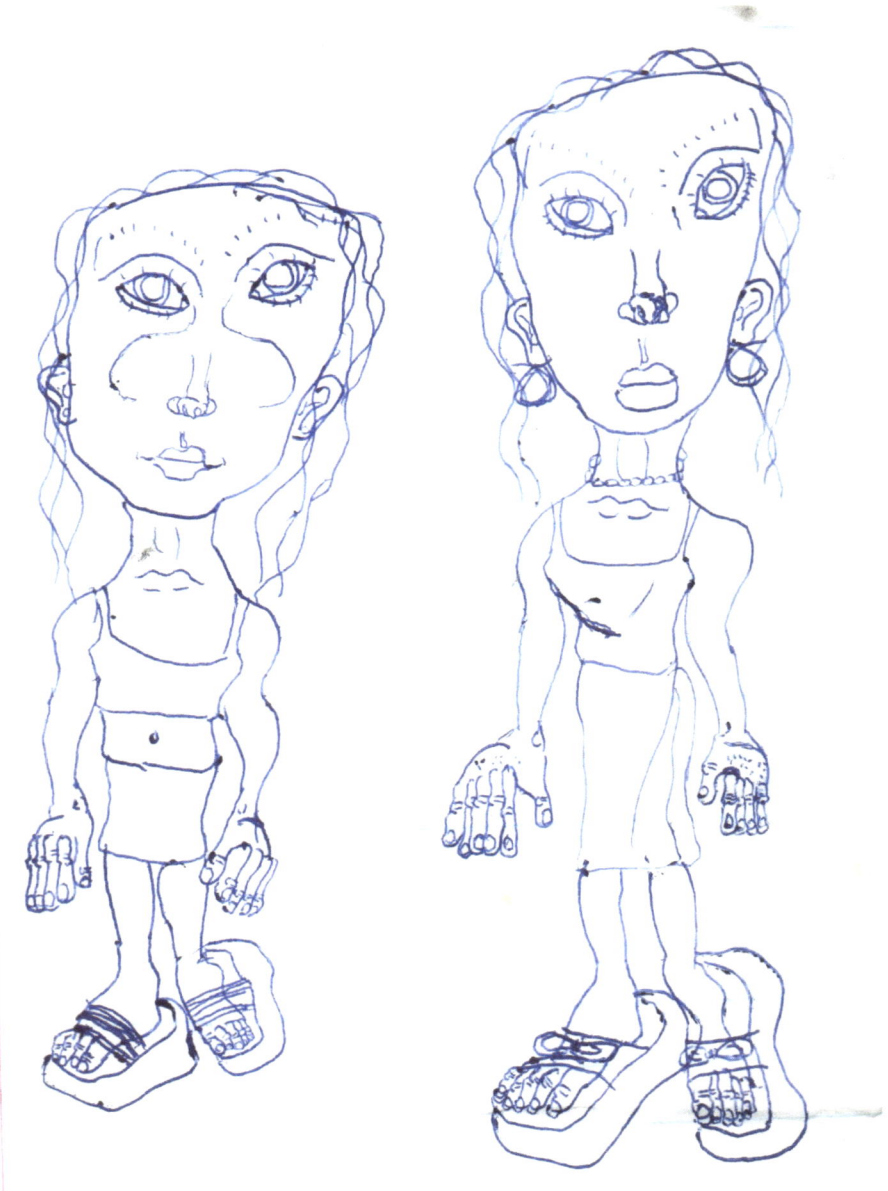

We are having a calm day.

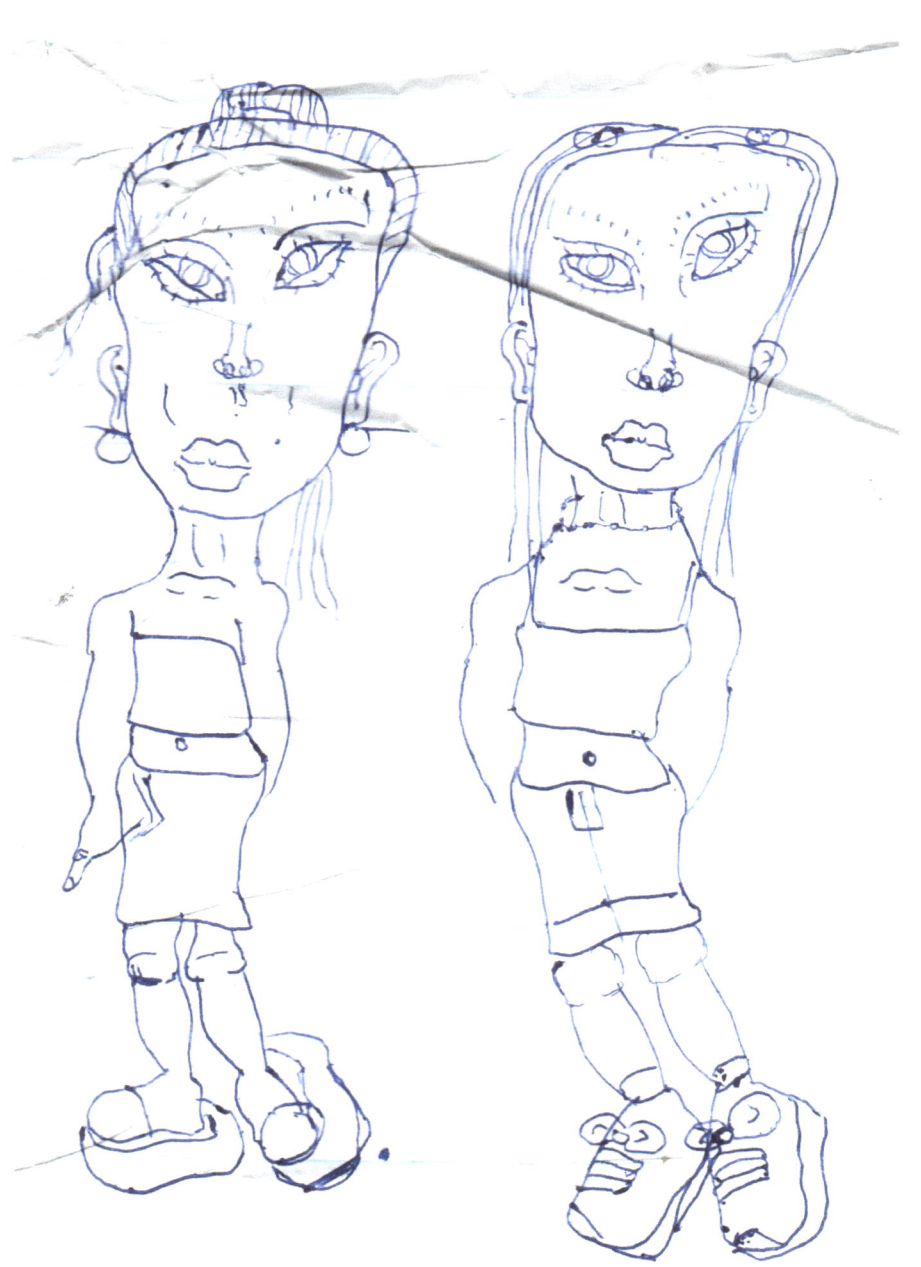

A little wrinkled, but having a good day!

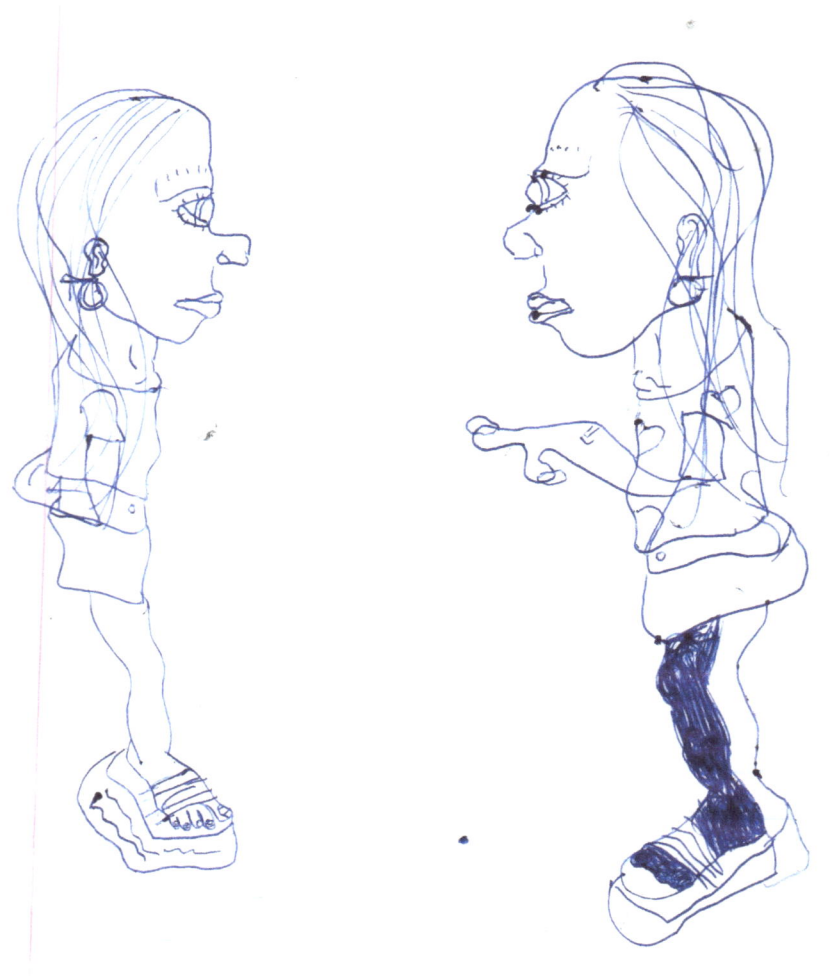

Did you hear about the new mall in town?

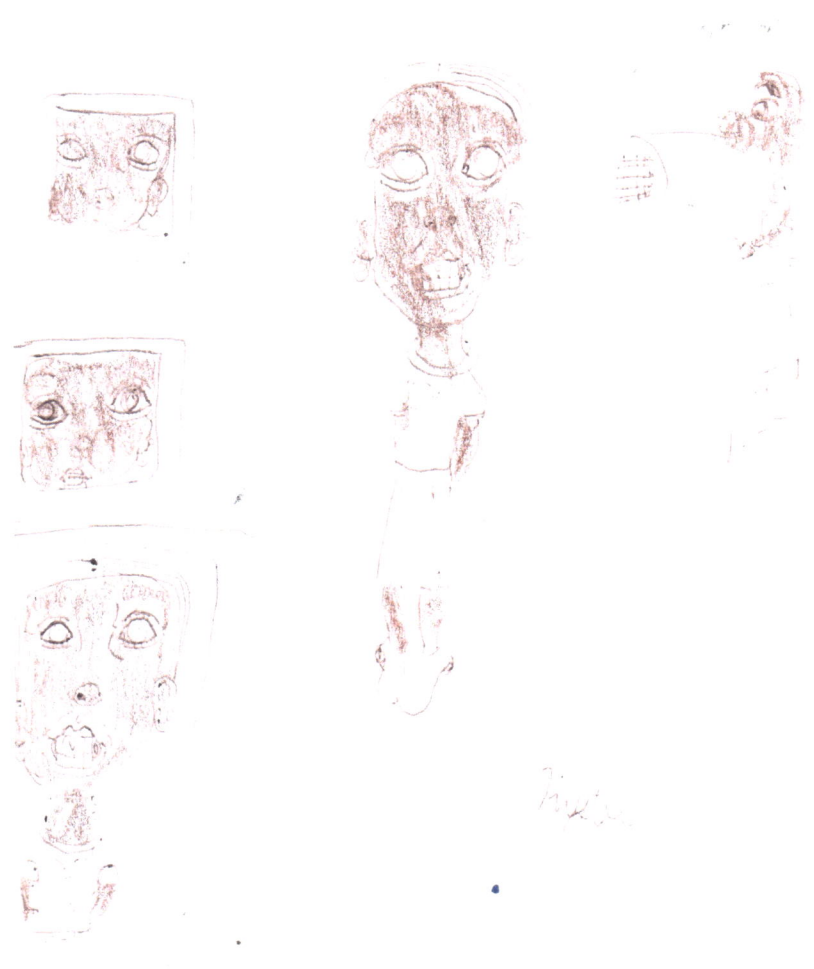

Original—I am on TV!

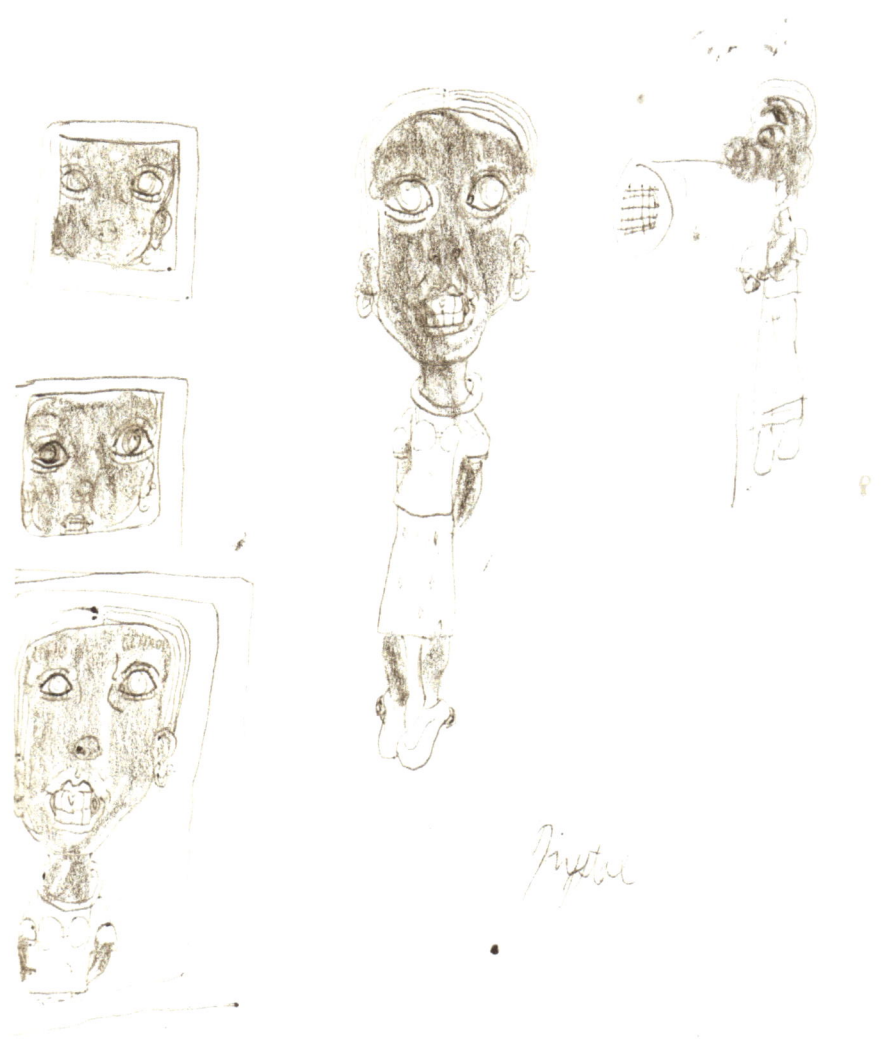

On TV in-Sepia Antique

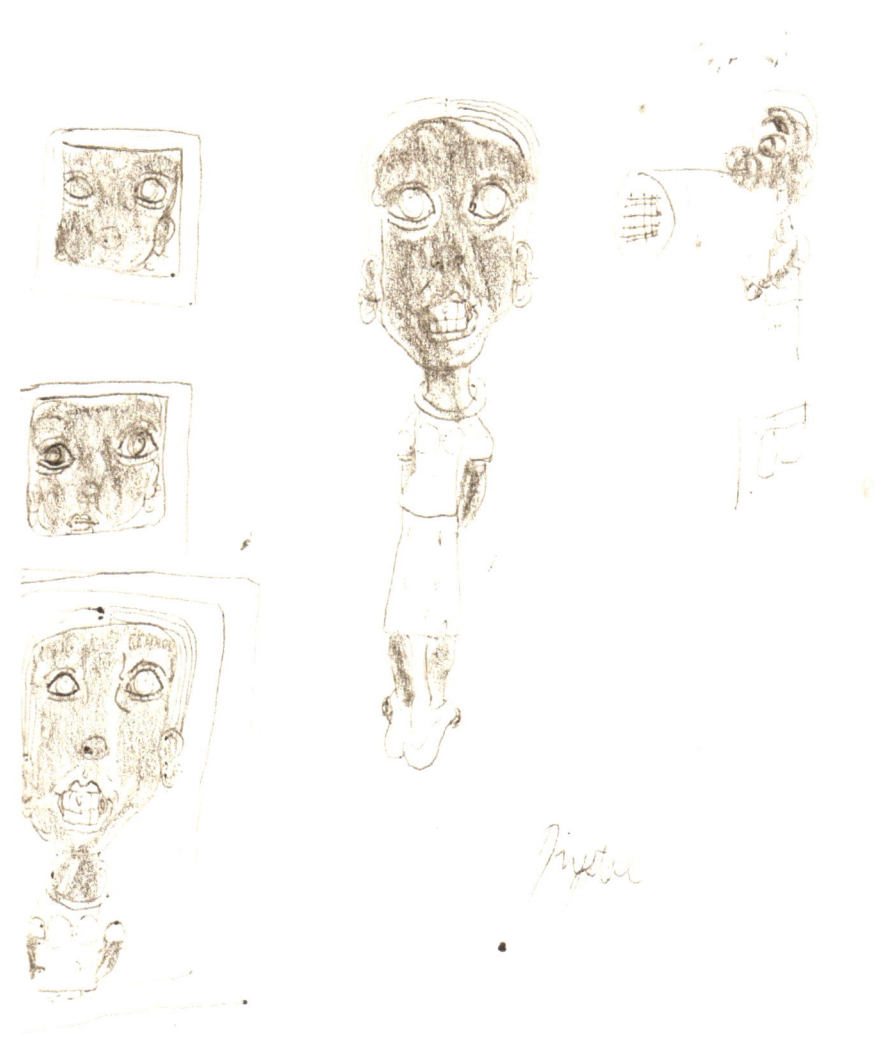

On TV in Brown Antique

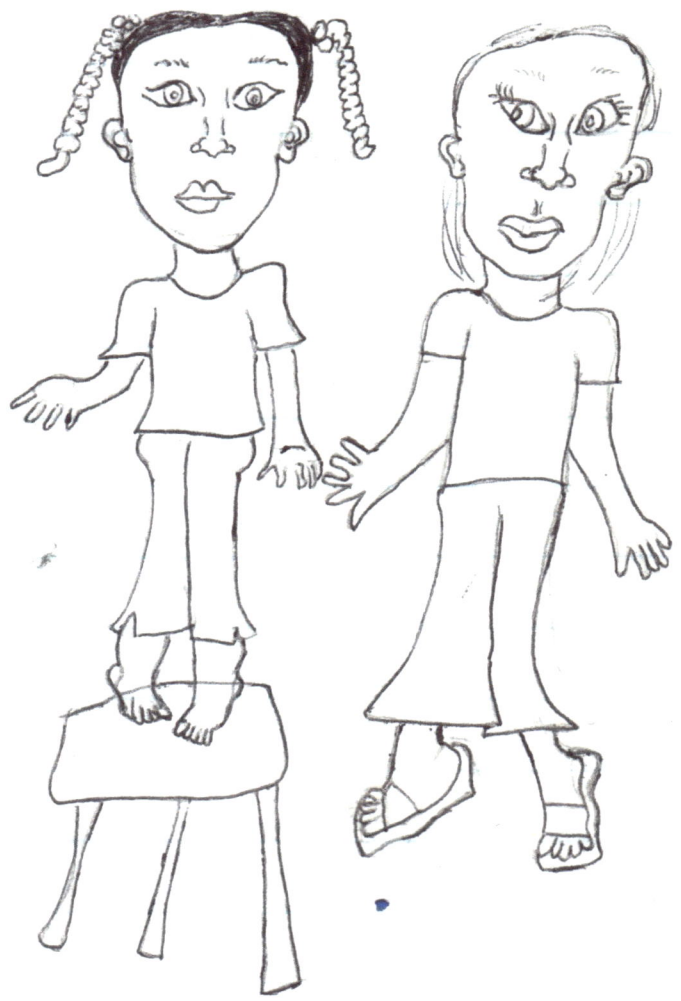

From cover-Friends just being friends….

Helpful Hints for Beginning Artists

1. Practice drawing every day.

2. Put objects on a table and try drawing them.

3. Crush a can and draw it.

4. Look at your hand and try drawing it.

5. Copy from pictures to practice.

6. Have someone sit for you and try drawing him or her.

7. Look outside and notice when the sun is bright and when the sun begins to go down.

8. What do the objects (outside) look like when the sun is brightest?

9. Where is the shade when the sun begins to go down? Paying attention to these details will help you to learn how to shade. Take pictures wherever you go so that you can practice paying attention to details.

10.   Buy colored pencils, charcoal pencils, acrylic paints and other types of arts and craft items. Practice with all of them until you realize which you like best.

11. Some Artists use a variety of items to develop their style and others know immediately what they like and stick with it.

12. Buy art books early so that you can study and practice.

13. Take art classes in class, correspondence and online.

14. Get to know as much as you can about art.

15. Learn the color wheel.

16. Enter Art Contests

17. Enjoy your art

18. Publish a book with your artwork.

19. Join an art club in your city and display your art.

Suggested online websites for free classes and other information & DVD's for sale

http://www.free-online-art-classes.com/

http://www.jerrysartarama.com/art-lessons/free-art-instruction-videos.html

http://www.artistsnetwork.com/online-video

http://www.artistsnetwork.com/category/competitions

http://thevirtualinstructor.com/freedrawinglessons.html
Free info. but fee for real lessons-over 300 good lessons-small fee for membership

http://www.acrylicpaintingsecrets.com/acrylic-painting-video1.html -free samples and some videos to order

http://www.artpromotivate.com/search/label/Art%20Promotion

http://thegluckmethod.com/howtodraw/courses/adultsartcourses.html

There are many other free art lessons listed online.

Correspondence courses

http://myarttv.com/ -fill in form online
http://www.interactiveartschool.com/

Possible Art careers with math or without math

architect, graphic artist, computer web designer, photographer, interior designer, wedding planner, cake decorator, engineer, painter, animator, chef, designer (clothes), set designer (for movies, plays etc.), sculptor and many more.....

Website for self publishing-which is really free to get started

www.createspace.com

Your journey as an artist is just beginning. Enjoy creating beautiful artwork for the rest of your life! Always remember that giving up is not an option!

About the Artist

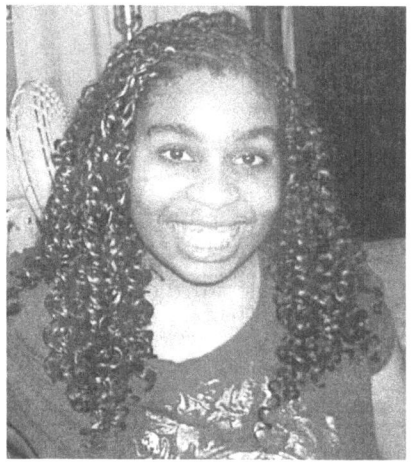

Krystal Liburd has been drawing since Pre-school. She is now a young adult who believes that art has made and is still making a difference in her life. Krystal has taken ballet, tap and dance, but her greatest love is art and math. She has also participated in two on stage productions. It is her desire to get on a television sitcom someday. It is also her hope that these pictures will bless all those who view them.

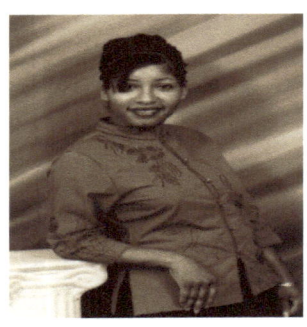 About the Writer

Faithe Reid-Liburd is a Conference Speaker and Teacher who believes that faith makes a difference. She has a Master's Degree in Education. As Krystal's mom, it has been her pleasure to help Krystal to publish her artwork.

Buy other books on Amazon.com
www.faithwithvision.com

Emancipation Proclamation: 150 years and Counting January 2013

Emancipation Proclamation: 150 years and Counting 2013 School Edition

What Do I Do When My Life Turns Upside Down? : Life Lessons From the Book of Ruth   January 2013

What Do I Do When My Life Turns Upside Down: Life Lessons From the Book of Ruth   (Study Companion) 2013

Silly Bailly
Four Children's Stories in 1 Volume
**   by Krystal Liburd   April 2013**

Express Yourself in Poetry 2013

Dreams Do Come True! An Inspirational Novella –
December 2013

A Tsunami Tale: A Story and Handbook on Grief -
2013

A Tsunami Tale: A Story and Handbook on Grief -
2013   School Edition

34 Scriptures That Remind Us to Give God Thanks
2014

I Have Confidence: I Walk By Faith   2014

I Love Art-Book 1-The Beginning –
                    Krystal Liburd 2014

To book Evangelist /Chaplain Faithe Reid–Liburd for a
speaking engagement, please contact her via the
website.

www.faithwithvision.com or via Facebook.com –
Evangelist Reid

Or write P.O. Box 830362, Ocala, FL 34483

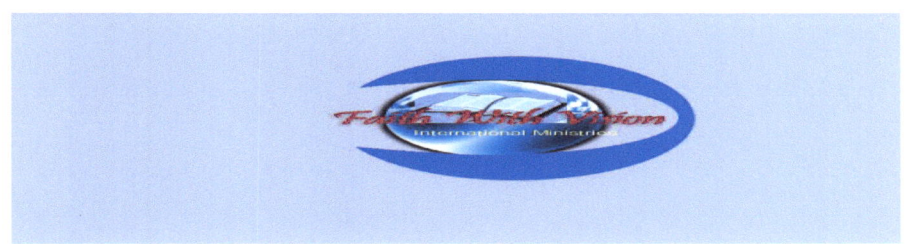

www.ingramcontent.com/pod-product-compliance
Lightning Source LLC
Chambersburg PA
CBHW040928180526
45159CB00002BA/659